AAT Technician Unit 17
Implementing Audit Procedures
(NVQ and Diploma Pathway)

Fourth edition May 2006

ISBN 0 7517 2626 5 (Previous edition 07517 2369 X)

British Library Cataloguing-in-Publication Data

A catalogue record for this book is available from the British Library

Published by

BPP Professional Education, Aldine House, Aldine Place, London W12 8AW

www.bpp.com

Printed in Great Britain by Ashford Colour Press

Welcome to BPP's AAT **Passcards**.

- They **save you time**. Important topics are summarised for you.

- They incorporate **diagrams** to kick start your memory.

- They follow the overall **structure** of the BPP Course Companions, but BPP's AAT **Passcards** are not just a condensed book. Each card has been separately designed for clear presentation. Topics are self contained and can be grasped visually.

- AAT **Passcards** are still **just the right size** for pockets, briefcases and bags.

- AAT **Passcards focus on the assessment** you will be facing.

- **AAT Passcards focus on the essential points** that you need to know in the workplace, or when completing your skills-based test.

Run through the complete set of **Passcards** as often as you can during your final revision period. The day before the assessment, try to go through the **Passcards** again! You will then be well on your way to completing your exam successfully.

Good luck!

The BPP **Revision Companion** contains activities and assessments that provide invaluable practice in the skills you need to complete this unit successfully.

1: The business environment

Topic List

Overview

Financial records

Audit

This chapter provides an introduction to audit and is the foundation for the rest of your studies.

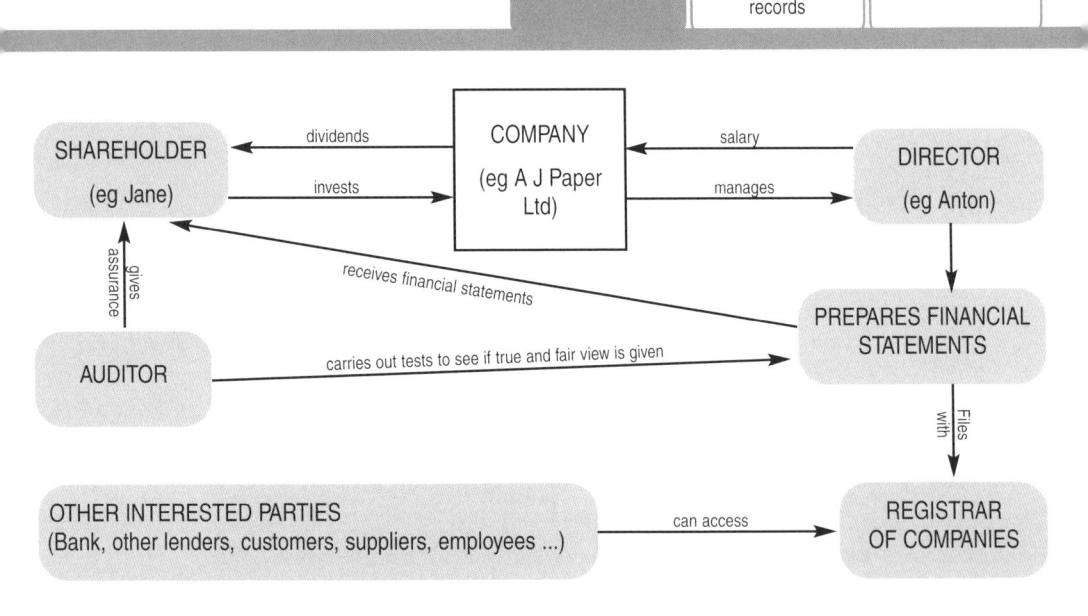

Every company must keep financial records to enable them to:

(1) disclose the financial position of the company at that time

(2) enable directors to ensure any balance sheet or profit and loss account prepared complies with the Act (Companies Act 1985)

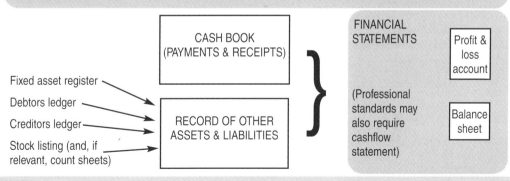

CASH BOOK
(PAYMENTS & RECEIPTS)

FINANCIAL STATEMENTS

Profit & loss account

Fixed asset register

Debtors ledger

Creditors ledger

Stock listing (and, if relevant, count sheets)

RECORD OF OTHER ASSETS & LIABILITIES

(Professional standards may also require cashflow statement)

Balance sheet

Audit

... tests and enquiries and judgements made by the auditors to come to a conclusion as to whether the financial statements show a true and fair view.

Requirement

The Companies Act 1985 requires

ALL COMPANIES TO HAVE AN AUDIT

Various other entities, such as housing associations, trade unions and charities are required to have audits under other statutes

Exemptions

- Small companies (Turnover ≤ £5.6m, Balance sheet ≤ £2.8m)

- Small charities that are companies (Gross income ≤ £250,000, Balance sheet ≤ £1.4m)

- Dormant companies

Report

Auditors are required to write a report to shareholders. It must express an opinion whether the financial statements:

- show a true and fair view

- of the state of affairs at year end, and

- of the profit or loss for the year

2: Introduction to audit

Topic List

Audit report

Law

Liability

Professional standards

Professional behaviour

Audit documentation

Engagement letter

The law and professional standards determine what the audit report must contain. This chapter contains essential background knowledge about the regulation of auditing.

*The law gives certain parties rights in the event of the auditors carelessly making a mistake. This is under the law of **negligence.***

Auditing standards require that auditors document the work they do in working papers. Working papers will be maintained in audit files.

Non-publicly traded company incorporated in Great Britain

Independent auditor's report to the shareholders of XYZ Limited

We have audited the financial statements of (name of entity) for the year ended ... which comprise [state the primary financial statement such as the Profit and Loss Account, the Balance Sheet, the Cash Flow Statement, the Statement of Total Recognised Gains and Losses] and the related notes. These financial statements have been prepared under the accounting policies set out therein.

Respective responsibilities of directors and auditors

The directors' responsibilities for preparing the Annual Report and the financial statements in accordance with applicable law and United Kingdom Accounting Standards (United Kingdom Generally Accepted Accounting Practice) are set out in the Statement of Directors' Responsibilities.

Our responsibility is to audit the financial statements in accordance with relevant legal and regulatory requirements and International Standards on Auditing (UK and Ireland).

We report to you our opinion as to whether the financial statements give a true and fair view and are properly prepared in accordance with the Companies Act 1985. We also report to you if, in our opinion, the Directors' Report is not consistent with the financial statements, if the company has not kept proper accounting records, if we have not received all the information and explanations we require for our audit, or if information specified by law regarding directors' remuneration and other transactions is not disclosed.

We read other information contained in the Annual Report, and consider whether it is consistent with the audited financial statements. This other information comprises only [the **Directors' Report, the Chairman's Statement and the Operating and Financial Review**]. We consider the implications for our report if we become aware of any apparent misstatements or material inconsistencies with the financial statements. Our responsibilities do not extend to any other information.

Basis of audit opinion

We conducted our audit in accordance with International Standards on Auditing (UK and Ireland) issued by the Auditing Practices Board. An audit includes examination, on a test basis, of evidence relevant to the amounts and disclosures in the financial statements. It also includes an assessment of the significant estimates and judgements made by the directors in the preparation of the financial statements, and of whether the accounting policies are appropriate to the company's circumstances, consistently applied and adequately disclosed.

We planned and performed our audit so as to obtain all the information and explanations which we consider necessary in order to provide us with sufficient evidence to give reasonable assurance that the financial statements are free from material misstatement, whether caused by fraud or other irregularity or error. In forming our opinion we also evaluated the overall adequacy of the presentation of information in the financial statements.

Opinion

In our opinion the financial statements:
- give a true and fair view, in accordance with United Kingdom Generally Accepted Accounting Practice, of the state of the company's affairs as at ... and of its profit (loss) for the year then ended; and
- have been properly prepared in accordance with the Companies Act 1985

Registered auditors   *Address*
Date

The directors could include a statement like this in the annual report:

> The directors are responsible for preparing the Annual Report and the Financial Statements in accordance with applicable law and United Kingdom Generally Accepted Accounting Practice. Company law requires the directors to prepare financial statements for each financial year which give a true and fair view of the state of affairs of the company and of the profit or loss of the company for that period. In preparing those financial statements, the directors are required to:
>
> (a) Select suitable accounting policies and then apply them consistently
> (b) Make judgements and estimates that are reasonable and prudent
> (c) State whether applicable accounting standards have been followed, subject to any material departures disclosed and explained in the financial statements (large companies only)
> (d) Prepare the financial statements on the going concern basis unless it is inappropriate to presume that the company will continue in business (if not separate statement on going concern is made by the directors)
>
> The directors are responsible for keeping proper accounting records which disclose with reasonable accuracy at any time the financial position of the company and to enable them to ensure that the financial statements comply with the Companies Act 1985. They are also responsible for safeguarding the assets of the company and hence for taking reasonable steps for the prevention and detection of fraud and other irregularities.

If the directors do not include such a statement in their annual report, the auditors must include it in their audit report.

Eligibility as an auditor

Must:

- be a member of an RSB
- hold an appropriate qualification

Recognised Supervisory Bodies

(RSBs) are bodies established in the UK, which maintain and enforce rules as to:

- eligibility of persons seeking to be auditors
- conduct of company audit work

Ineligibility as an auditor

Under the Companies Act, cannot be:

- an officer or employee of the company
- a partner or employee of the above
- a partnership in which the above is partner
- any of the above in a subsidiary company

RSBs must have rules to ensure correct people are deemed eligible to undertake company audits.

They must also maintain the competence of members and monitor compliance.

The law does not make ineligible a shareholder or debtor/creditor of a company or a close relative of an officer/employee. However, these would be excluded by most RSBs. The law does state that someone can be ineligible through 'lack of independence', which is not otherwise defined at the moment.

Appointment

The auditor is appointed by the shareholders. In practice, the following situation arises:

AUDIT FIRM

tenders to

DIRECTORS

make recommendation to

SHAREHOLDERS

Appoint

Rights

The law gives auditors certain rights.

Auditors' rights
A right of access to books/vouchers.
A right to require information and explanations from company officers.
A right to attend company general meetings, to be heard on matters concerning them as auditors, to receive copies of written resolutions, to require a meeting to give shareholders the accounts.

CONTRACT

- **Express** – engagement letter

- **Implied terms** – law implies terms into such contracts for services.

Three things must exist for a successful negligence claim:

(a) **Duty of care**
There existed a duty of care enforceable at law.

Under a **contract** this is always the case

(b) **Negligence**
In a situation where a duty of care existed, the auditors were negligent in the performance of that duty, judged by the accepted professional standards of the day.

(c) **Damages**
The client has suffered some monetary loss as a direct consequence of the negligence on the part of the auditors.

Professional standards of care include using generally accepted auditing techniques (auditing standards), carrying out investigations until the auditor is satisfied, acting honestly and carefully when making judgements.

Third parties do not have a contract with the audit firm, so there is **no automatic duty of care**.

The three elements for a successful negligence claim are the same:

(a) **Duty of care**
There existed a duty of care enforceable at law

> Without a **contract**, this may not be the case

> The key issue for a third party to prove is that a duty of care exists. Case law has implied in the past that auditors do not owe third parties a duty of care.

(b) **Negligence**
In a situation where a duty of care existed, the auditors were negligent in the performance of that duty, judged by the accepted professional standards of the day.

> However, if the auditor knows a third party is relying and he doesn't disclaim liability, he may be found to have a duty of care to that person/entity.

(c) **Damages**
The client has suffered some monetary loss as a direct consequence of the negligence on the part of the auditors.

In the UK the Auditing Practices Board (APB) is responsible for issuing auditing standards and guidance.

These include the following types of pronouncements:

- International Standards on Quality Control (ISQCs)
- International Standards on Auditing (ISAs)
- Practice notes
- Bulletins

ISQCs/ISAs

Contain basic principles and essential procedures. These must be applied in the context of the explanatory and other material

Practice Notes

These assist the auditor in applying ISAs of general application

Bulletins

These provide auditors with timely guidance on new and emerging issues

Strictly speaking ISAs issued by the APB should be referred to as ISAs (UK and Ireland). In these Passcards we will simply refer to them as ISAs.

- Persuasive, not prescriptive
- Indicative of good practice

FUNDAMENTAL PRINCIPLES	
Integrity	Members should be straightforward and honest in performing professional work.
Objectivity	Members should be fair and should not allow prejudice or bias or the influence of others to override objectivity.
Professional and technical competence	Members should not undertake work they are not competent to do unless they receive advice or assistance. They also have a continuing duty to maintain their technical knowledge - developments in practice, legislation and techniques and Continuing Professional Development.
Due care	A member has an obligation to carry out work with due care. Special care is needed where the client has little knowledge of accounting or tax matters.
Confidentiality	Members should respect the confidentiality of information given to them and not disclose it unless there is specific authority, or legal or professional right to do so.
Professional behaviour	Members should act in a manner consistent with the good reputation of the profession and refrain from discreditable conduct.

Confidentiality

Auditors have a duty to respect the confidentiality of the client's affairs, except in certain circumstances.

1 **Authorised disclosure**. Where the client gives permission. (Consider the effects on all third parties)

2 **Disclosure required by law**. This could lead to a member providing documents to a court of law, or disclosing infringements of law to the authorities.

3 **Professional duty to disclose**. To comply with technical standards, to protect the interests of the member, to respond to an enquiry by the AAT.

Security procedures

- Do not discuss client matters with any third party (even family)
- Do not use client information to your own gain
- Do not leave audit files unattended at the client's premises
- Do not leave audit cases in cars, or in unsecured private residences
- Do not take working papers away from the office without good reason

When making legal disclosure, the member should consider three things: whether all the relevant facts are known and substantiated, what type of communication is required and whether the member would incur any legal liability having made the communication.

Independence

Auditors are to give an impartial opinion. It is therefore important that they are independent of the company.

Quality standards require firms to put safeguards into place to prevent loss of independence through these factors.

ISA 220 requires the audit engagement partner to take responsibility for the independence and objectivity of the audit team and firm.

Audit firms should not accept appointment in the first place if there are significant barriers to independence.

Threats to independence

- Loans to/from clients
- One client is high proportion of fee income
- Family or other close relationships with management
- Holding shares in clients (directly/indirectly)
- Accepting gifts/hospitality from company
- Having fees outstanding (like a loan)

Guidance is given in ISA 230 *Audit Documentation*.

Auditors should document in their working papers matters which are important in supporting their report. There are three areas which you must consider:

1. **Form and content of working papers**
2. **Ownership and confidentiality**
3. **Review**

Working papers

The material the auditors prepare or obtain and retain in connection with the performance of the audit

1. Form and content

Partner needs to be able to satisfy himself that all planned work has been carried out.

Document what would be necessary for an experienced auditor to understand work done and conclusions drawn without client knowledge.

You should learn the details which working papers should contain (eg headers/dates).

2. Ownership

Audit WPs belong to auditor.

3. Review

When work has been carried out by the audit team, there will be a manager review and a partner review. The reviewer will initial reviewed pages.

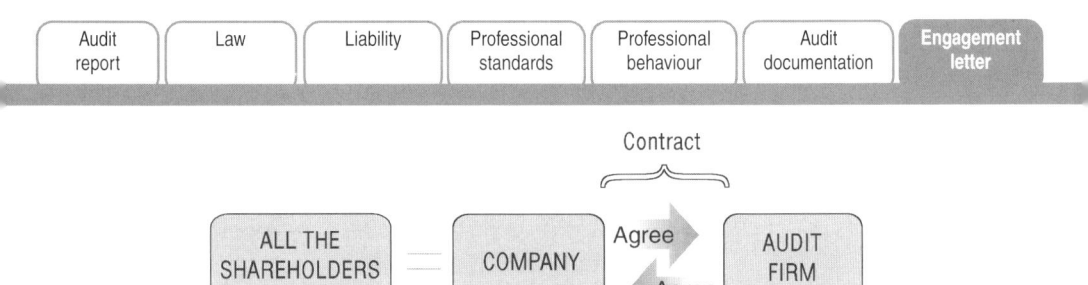

Auditing standards require auditors to set out the express terms of the contract with the client in writing, in what is known as an **engagement letter**. This should prevent misunderstanding between client and audit firm. If the terms of the engagement change for any reason, or it becomes clear the client misunderstands the terms of the engagement, a new engagement letter should be issued.

Items which might be included in an engagement letter include:

Fees

Billing arrangements

Complaints procedures

Liability

Use of other auditors/ experts

Relevant law

Timetable

3-4: Controls and auditing systems

Topic List

Internal control

Tests of controls

Control activities

CAATs

Reporting to management

Auditors must gain an understanding of the accounting system and internal control. The auditors may decide to carry out an audit that relies on the systems of the client, in which case they will carry out tests of controls. If these produce good results, the auditor can then reduce substantive procedures. The auditor may use CAATs to assist in this work.

A common by-product of this process is a report to management, also sometimes called a letter of weakness or management letter.

Internal control is the process designed and effected by those charged with governance, management and other personnel, to provide reasonable assurance about the achievement of the entity's objectives with regard to reliability of financial reporting, effectiveness and efficiency of operations and compliance with applicable laws and regulations.

Components of internal control

- Control environment
- Risk assessment process
- The information system
- Control activities
- Monitoring of controls

Relevant controls

Not all controls are relevant to the auditor's risk assessment. The auditor is primarily concerned with those which are part of the management of risk that may give rise to a material misstatement in the FS.

Control environment

The attitudes, awareness and actions of management.

- Communication and enforcement of integrity and ethical values
- Commitment to competence
- Participation by those charged with governance
- Management's philosophy and operating style
- Organisational structure
- Assignment of authority and responsibility
- Human resource policies and practices

Risk assessment process

The process of identifying and responding to business risk.

Risk can arise due to:

- changes in operating environment
- new personnel
- new/revamped information systems
- rapid growth
- new technology
- new business models, products or activities
- corporate restructuring
- expanded foreign operations
- new accounting pronouncements

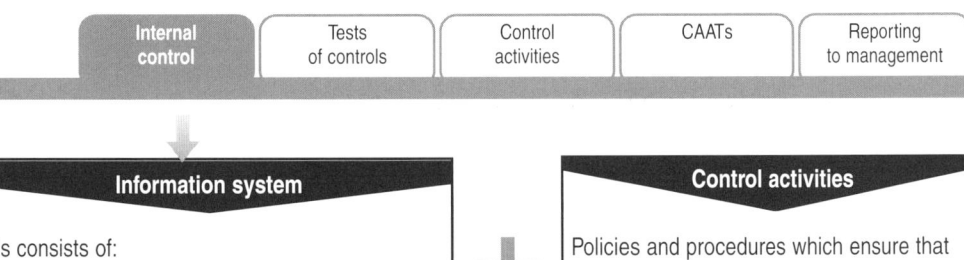

Information system

This consists of:
- infrastructure (physical/hardware)
- software
- people
- procedures
- data

The IS relevant to FR objectives **initiates**, **records**, **processes** and **reports** transactions

Control activities

Policies and procedures which ensure that management directives are carried out.
- Performance reviews
- Information processing
- Physical controls
- Segregation of duties

Monitoring of controls

A process to asses the quality of internal control performance over time
- Operating as intended/modified as appropriate
- Internal audit may perform part of this function

An internal control system only provides directors with **reasonable** assurance that objectives are met because any internal control system has **inherent limitations.**

- Costs of control outweigh the benefit
- Potential for **human error**
- Possibility of collusion in fraud between employees
- Controls could be bypassed/overridden by management
- Controls are designed to cope with routine transactions not non-routine ones

> Hence segregation of duties is vital

Assessment of systems

The auditors must gain an understanding of the accounting system so that they can understand the **major classes of transaction, how** transactions are **initiated**, what the **significant records** are, and what the **financial reporting process** is.

A record of the system will be made. Methods include:

- narrative notes
- flow charts
- ICQs
- checklists

Statutory requirements

The directors of a company are required by law to keep accounting records which disclose with reasonable accuracy the affairs of the company at any stated time.

The auditors assess whether the system allows the directors to carry out this duty.

Walkthrough testing

Walk-through tests involve tracing one or more transactions through the system and observing the application of the control system on the transactions

The auditors will **ascertain** the system from previous years' notes and from discussions with management and staff. However, it is vital to **ensure that the system operates as has been stated**. So a walk-through test is undertaken.

Control risk assessment

Once the system has been walked-through, the auditors can make a preliminary assessment of **control risk**. We will look at risk assessment in Chapter 5.

Tests of controls

Performed when the risk assessment includes an expectation of their operating effectiveness or when substantive procedures alone are insufficient

Tests of controls may include:

- **enquiries** about and **observation** of control activities (procedures)
- **inspection** of documents supporting controls
- **examination of evidence of management views**
- **reperformance** of control activities to ensure they were correctly performed
- **testing** of controls operating on specific **computer applications**

If risk assessment has shown controls to be ineffective testing will not be undertaken. It may also be **inefficient** to test controls if the population consists of a few large items which can be tested quickly by substantive tests.

When controls testing is completed, auditors make a final assessment of control risk, and **revise** the nature, timing & extent of **substantive procedures** accordingly.

Auditors should consider: **how** controls were applied, **how consistently** they were applied and **by whom**. Controls testing is often completed on an **interim audit**.

Auditors should **combine** enquiry with another type of procedure when testing controls.

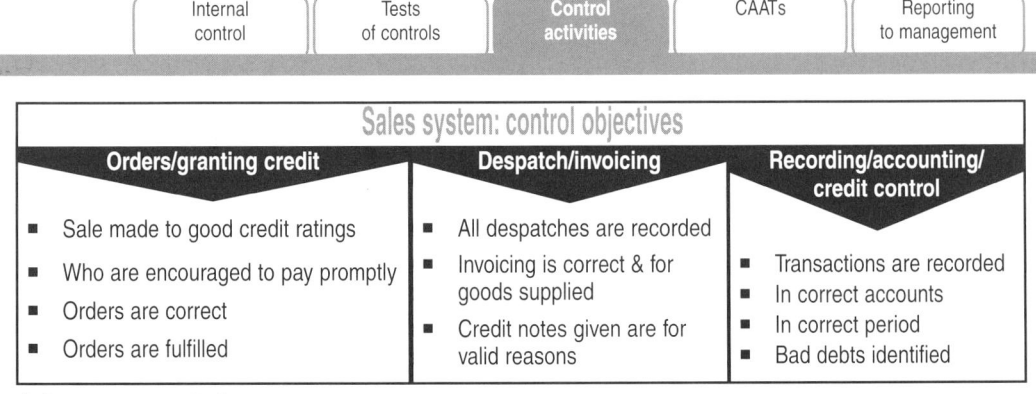

Sales system: control objectives

Orders/granting credit	Despatch/invoicing	Recording/accounting/credit control
■ Sale made to good credit ratings ■ Who are encouraged to pay promptly ■ Orders are correct ■ Orders are fulfilled	■ All despatches are recorded ■ Invoicing is correct & for goods supplied ■ Credit notes given are for valid reasons	■ Transactions are recorded ■ In correct accounts ■ In correct period ■ Bad debts identified

Sales system controls

Ordering/granting credit

- Segregation of duties (credit control/invoice/despatch)
- Authorisation of credit terms (checks obtained review)
- Sequential numbering of pre-printed order forms
- Correct prices quoted to customers
- Match orders to despatch notes (o/s orders queried)
- Dealing with customer queries

Tests of controls

Check for evidence of:

- references
- authorisation
- credit terms/limits
- matching orders

Despatch/invoicing

- Authorisation of despatch
- Examination of goods despatched (quality)
- Recording of goods outward
- Match despatch notes to order/invoice (o/s queried)
- Sequential numbering of pre-printed despatch notes
- Signature of customer on delivery notes
- Authorisation of price on invoice (price list)
- Arithmetical checks on invoices

Verify details of sales invoices with despatch notes

Test numerical sequences of records (enquire about gaps)

Verify invoices to stock records

Accounting/recording/credit control

- Segregation of duties (recording sales/statements)
- Recording of sequence of sales invoices
- Matching cash receipts with invoices
- Retention of customer remittance advices
- Preparation/checking of debtors' statements
- Review/chase overdue accounts/authorised write off
- Reconciliation off sales control account

Check entries in day book to invoices, check additions and postings to ledgers

Check entries in ledger, scrutinise for credit limits, check debtors' statements, check that reconciliations performed

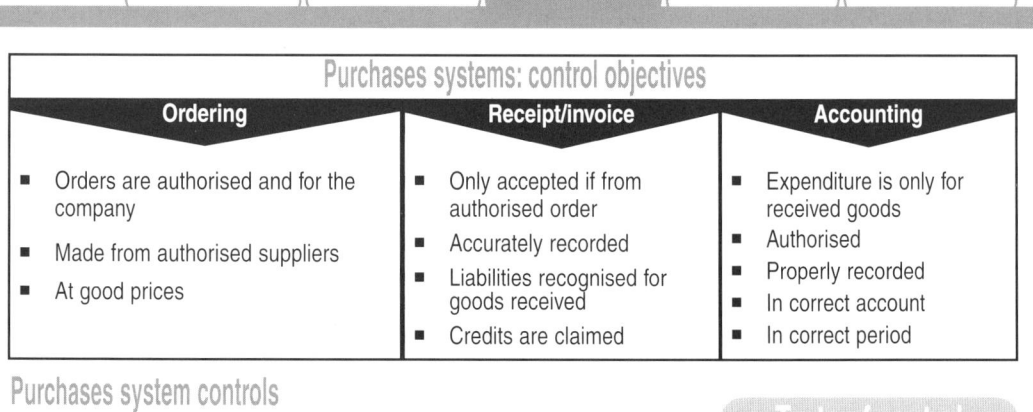

Purchases systems: control objectives

Ordering	**Receipt/invoice**	**Accounting**
■ Orders are authorised and for the company ■ Made from authorised suppliers ■ At good prices	■ Only accepted if from authorised order ■ Accurately recorded ■ Liabilities recognised for goods received ■ Credits are claimed	■ Expenditure is only for received goods ■ Authorised ■ Properly recorded ■ In correct account ■ In correct period

Purchases system controls

Ordering
- Segregation of duties (requisitioning/ordering)
- Central policy for choice of supplier
- Use of pre-numbered purchase requisitions
- Authorised, pre-numbered (safeguarded) order forms
- Monitoring of supplier terms for most favourable

Tests of control

It is vital that auditors check that all invoices are supported by genuine purchase orders, authorised by correct individual.

Goods received

- Examine goods inwards (quality) and record deliveries
- Compare goods received notes (GRNs) with orders
- Reference suppliers' invoices
- Check suppliers' invoices (maths, prices, quantities)
- Record goods returns
- Have procedures for obtaining credit notes

Accounting

- Segregation of duties (recording/checking)
- Prompt recording in day books and ledgers
- Comparison of supplier statements to ledger accounts
- Authorisation of payments (limits/goods received)
- Review of allocation of expenditure
- Reconciliation of purchase ledger with total of balances
- Procedures for cut off

Check invoices are supported by GRNs, priced correctly, coded correctly, entered in stock, maths correct, posted to ledger

Check numerical sequences

Check that purchase day book adds and is referenced to invoices

Check entries to ledger

Check control account reconciled/no unusual entries

Cash system: control objectives

- All monies received are banked, recorded and safeguarded against loss/theft
- All payments are authorised, made out to the correct payees, recorded
- Payments are not made twice for the same liability

Cash system controls

Receipts

- Segregation of duties
- Safeguards at post opening (2 people/listing)
- Post stamped with date of receipt
- Restrictions on receipt of cash (salespeople only)
- Agreement of cash collections to till rolls
- Prompt maintenance of records
- Giving and recording receipts for cash

Tests of controls

Observe post opening. Trace entries on listing to cash book, paying in book, bank statement

Verify till receipts to cash sale summaries, check to paying in slip

Check cash is banked daily

Bank

- Daily bankings, banking of receipts intact
- Restrictions on opening new bank accounts
- Limitations on cash floats
- Surprise cash counts
- Custody of cash and cheques
- Restrictions on issuing blank cheques
- Bank reconciliations

Payments

- Cheque requisitions supported by documentation/authorised
- Authorised signatories
- Prompt despatch of signed cheques
- Payments recorded promptly
- Cash payments authorised
- Limit on disbursements
- Rules of cash advances to employees

Check cash receipts from cash book to paying in slips, bank, posting to the sales ledger, posting to the general ledger

For cash payments, check that cheques are signed by authorised signatories (paid cheques can be requested from the bank), check to supplier invoice, verify that supporting documents are stamped 'paid'. Check postings to the ledgers

Reperform a bank reconciliation

Observe a cash account

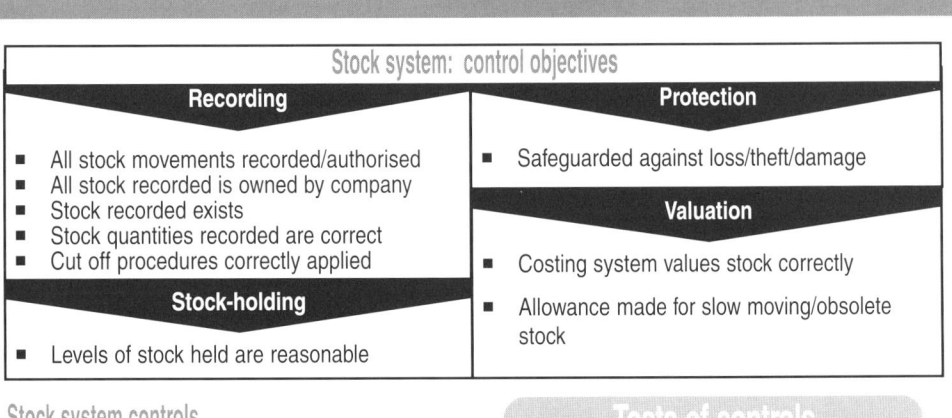

Stock system: control objectives

Recording

- All stock movements recorded/authorised
- All stock recorded is owned by company
- Stock recorded exists
- Stock quantities recorded are correct
- Cut off procedures correctly applied

Stock-holding

- Levels of stock held are reasonable

Protection

- Safeguarded against loss/theft/damage

Valuation

- Costing system values stock correctly
- Allowance made for slow moving/obsolete stock

Stock system controls

Recording

- Segregation of duties (custody/recording)
- Goods inwards met and checked
- Stock issues supported by documentation
- Stock records maintained

Tests of controls

Test check stock counts, ensure discrepancies are investigated, authorised and corrected

Stock taking is covered in Chapter 7

Protection

- Precautions against theft (restriction)
- Precautions against deterioration
- Security over stock held by third parties
- Regular stock taking

Valuation

- Valuation agrees with SSAP 9
- Calculations are checked
- Condition of stock is reviewed
- Accounting for waste is provided for

Stockholding

- Provision made for stock levels
- Minimum/maximum stock levels exist

Check a sample of stock records to goods received and goods despatched notes

Check sequence of stock records

Observe security arrangements for stocks

Consider the environment in which stocks are held

Wages system: control objectives

- Employees only paid authorised amounts for work done.
- Deductions are recorded and pay agrees to bank records.
- Correct employees are paid.
- Deductions are correct and paid over to the correct authorities.

Wages system controls

- Segregation of duties
- Authorisation
- Recording of any changes
- Custody of cash for cash payouts
- Maintenance of salary bank account
- Reconciliation of accounts
- Recording of payroll
- Reconciliations of deductions
- Surprise cash counts

Tests of controls

It is vital to check that all aspects of the payroll (amounts/deductions/payments) are authorised

Attend cash payouts to ensure controlled

Check payroll information to clock cards, timesheets. Check maths, check postings, check reconciliation with cash

It is now common for both businesses and auditors to use **computers**. IT brings many advantages to audit.

CAATs (Computer assisted audit techniques) are exactly what their name says. They are audit tests which are performed using computers, which can enhance the detail of the test undertaken and the result of the test.

Audit software	**Test data**
This performs checks that auditors would otherwise have had to do by hand.	This is a way of **checking whether systems are operating properly:** feed the system some data to see how it is processed.
Interrogation (data files)	The data may be valid or invalid, depending on the objective of the test.
Comparison (comparing versions)	
Interactive (on-line)	
Resident code (as transactions are processed)	

A report to management will highlight any weaknesses in controls and systems which the auditors have noted during the course of their audit.

It usually takes the form:

Weakness ➤ An outline of the problem

Consequence ➤ The implications that this will have for the business

Recommendation ➤ An idea to make the control work better, or an alternative control option

for each matter highlighted.

Auditors are also required to report certain matters to those charged with governance.

Those charged with governance

Those persons entrusted with the supervision, control and direction of an entity. Those charged with governance include the directors of a company or other body, the partners, proprietors, committee of management or trustees of other forms of entity, or equivalent persons responsible for directing the entity's affairs and preparing its financial statements.

Management

Those persons who have executive responsibility for the conduct of the entity's operations and the preparation of its financial statements

In writing or orally?

The auditors will be affected by such matters as:

- the size, operating structure, legal structure & communication process of the entity
- the nature, sensitivity and significance of the matters being communicated
- statutory and regulatory requirements
- the arrangements made re periodic meetings or reporting of significant matters

Matters which the communications should include are:

- information relating to the planning of the audit (materiality/approach)
- findings from the audit and their impact on the audit report
- unadjusted misstatements, and the reasons for them
- matters arising from ISAs, for example, law and regulations, fraud and error
- requirements for written representations
- relationships which affect the independence and objectivity of audit staff (particularly listed companies)

Matters should be discussed with those charged with governance on a sufficiently prompt basis that those people can react to what the auditor has said.

5: Assessing risks

Topic List

Understanding the entity

Audit risk

Materiality

Responding to risk

Fraud, law and regulation

Related parties

Risk assessment is an important topic area, so you should ensure that you understand and can explain all aspects of audit risk. You also need to be able to assess risks in any given scenario as this is an important performance criterion.

Considering the likelihood and impact of fraud is an important part of the risk assessment process.

Auditors should obtain an understanding of the entity and its environment, including its internal control, sufficient to identify and assess the risks of material misstatement of the FS whether due to fraud or error, and sufficient to design and perform further audit procedures.

Sources of information	Using the information
Previous experience of client/industry	Develop the audit strategy
Visits to the client's premises	Consider and assess risks
Discussions with staff/directors	Determine appropriate materiality
Discussions with previous auditors	Consider complexity of info systems
Discussions with other advisors	Identify special skills aspects of audit
Discussions with other external 3P	Assess appropriateness of evidence
Publications related to the industry	Evaluate accounting estimates
Legislation and regulations	Evaluate management representations
Documents produced by the client	Recognise conflicting information
Professional literature on industry	Make informed enquiries

AUDIT RISK   =   RISK OF MATERIAL MISSTATEMENT   +   DETECTION RISK

Inherent Risk   Control Risk

| Risk that the auditor expresses an inappropriate audit option

The auditor also needs to consider **business risk.** | The susceptability of an assertion to a misstatement that could be material, either individually or when aggregated with other misstatements, assuming that there are no related controls. | The risk that a misstatement that could occur in an assertion and that could be material, either individually or when aggregated with other misstatements will not be prevented, or detected and corrected on a timely basis by the entity's internal control. | The risk that the auditor will not detect a misstatement that exists in an assertion that could be material, either materially or when aggregated with other misstatements. |

- The auditor has no control over inherent and control risks, which are affected by the entity
- If the auditor's preliminary assessment includes an expectation that **controls** are **operating effectively, controls testing should be undertaken**.

Assessing risk

Auditors:

- assess the adequacy of the accounting system as the basis for the FS
- identify the types of potential misstatement that could occur
- consider factors that affect the risk of misstatements
- **design appropriate audit procedures**

Indication of significant risk per ISA 315

- Susceptibility to fraud
- Impact of recent developments
- Subjectivity of financial data

- Unusualness of transaction
- Related party impact
- Complexity of transaction

| Understanding the entity | Audit risk | **Materiality** | Responding to risk | Fraud, law and regulation | Related parties |

Materiality

Materiality is a measure of how important items and issues are and relates to the financial statements as a whole and to individual items.

> Auditors should consider materiality when determining the nature, timing and extent of the audit procedures.

> Materiality and detection risk are therefore linked.

Assessing materiality helps the auditor judge:

- what/how many items to test
- whether to use sampling techniques
- level of error leading to qualification of audit opinion

Items may be material due to:

- relative **size**
- their **nature** (eg directors' emoluments disclosures)

These should be reassessed during the audit owing to changes in accounts/risk assessments

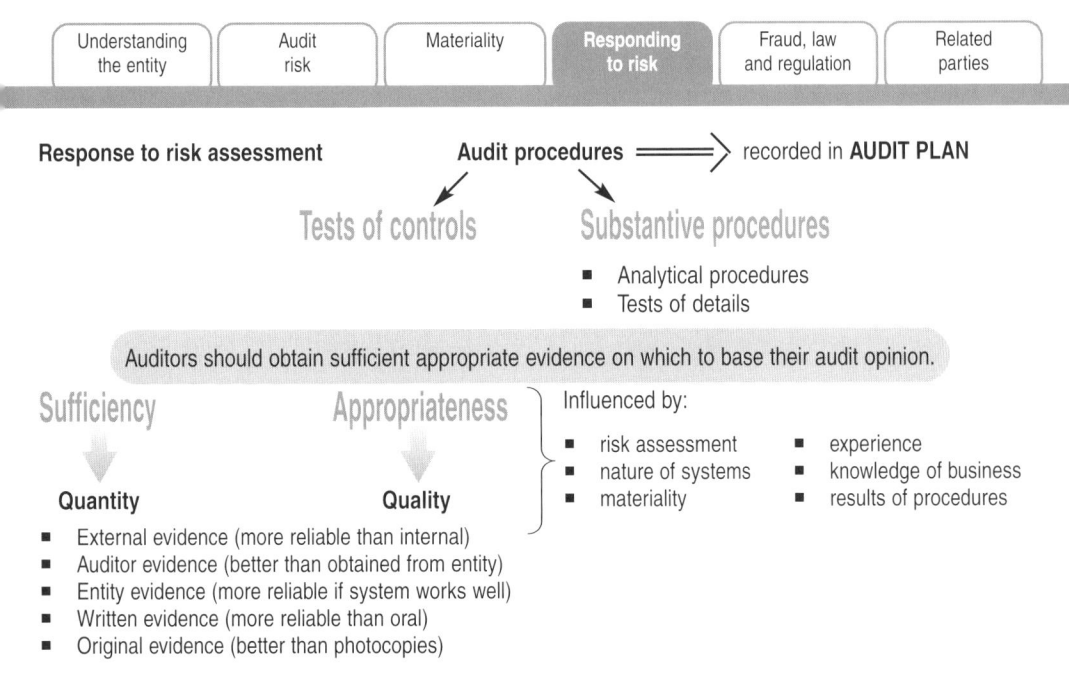

Response to risk assessment   Audit procedures ====> recorded in **AUDIT PLAN**

Tests of controls   Substantive procedures

- Analytical procedures
- Tests of details

Auditors should obtain sufficient appropriate evidence on which to base their audit opinion.

Sufficiency   Appropriateness   Influenced by:

- risk assessment   experience
- nature of systems   knowledge of business
- materiality   results of procedures

Quantity   Quality

- External evidence (more reliable than internal)
- Auditor evidence (better than obtained from entity)
- Entity evidence (more reliable if system works well)
- Written evidence (more reliable than oral)
- Original evidence (better than photocopies)

Tests of controls

Remember: The auditors need evidence about two aspects of the system:

- The **design** of the systems (capable of preventing/detecting misstatements?)
- The **operation** of the systems (have they existed/operated properly in the period?)

Role of controls testing

ISA 330 states that when an auditor's assessment of risks of material misstatement includes an expectation that **controls are operating effectively**, the auditor should **perform tests of controls** to obtain sufficient appropriate audit evidence that the controls were operating effectively at relevant times during the period under audit.

The message is that you cannot arbitrarily go down the substantive route in circumstances where there are effective controls from which audit assurance may be obtained.

Substantive procedures

The auditors are seeking to **substantiate assertions** made by the directors (known as the financial statement assertions) regarding transactions and events, account balances and disclosure.

Assertions

- About classes of transactions and events

  (occurence, completeness, accuracy, cut off, classification)

- About account balances at the period end

  (existence, rights and obligations (ownership), completeness, valuation and allocation)

- About presentation and disclosure

  (occurence and rights and obligations, completeness, classification and understandability, accuracy and valuation)

Evidence about the assertion is obtained through the following **procedures**.

- **Inspection** of assets
- **Inspection** of documentation
- **Observation**
- **Enquiries**
- **Confirmation**
- **Recalculation/reperformance**
- **Analytical procedures**

An auditor must always carry out substantive procedures on material items. An audit can never only be based on tests of controls.

ISA 520 *Analytical procedures* gives guidance.

1. **Nature and purpose of analytical procedures**
2. **Risk assessment procedures**
3. **Overall review**
4. **Significant fluctuations/unexpected relationships**

1. Analytical procedures include:

Comparisons of this year's financial information with:

- similar information for prior periods
- anticipated results/budgets
- industry information

Elements of financial information which are **expected to conform** to patterns

Links between financial / non financial information

Analytical procedures

The analysis of relationships between items of data and relevant information

2. Risk assessment procedures

Analytical procedures should be used as risk assessment procedures to obtain an understanding of the entity and its environment.

Sources of information:

- Interim financial information
- Budget/management accounts
- Non-financial information
- Bank records/VAT returns
- Board minutes
- Discussions with directors

3. Overall review (see Chapter 10)

Analytical procedures should also used to ensure the FS seem reasonable at final review. The results should be consistent with other audit evidence gained.

4. Significant fluctuations/unexpected relationships

When these are identified, the auditors will:

- make enquiries of directors

- consider management response in light of knowledge/evidence

- carry out additional audit procedures where necessary

Practical techniques are also important.

Auditors will use the primary **accounting ratios** (you should be familiar with these). There are also a number of significant relationships in FS:

> Creditors/purchases   stocks/cost of sales,
> fixed assets/depreciation/repairs expense
> intangible assets/amortisation
> loans/interest expense
> investments/investment income
> debtors/bad debt expense/sales

Steps to take if fraud or non-compliance with law/regulations is suspected:

Step 1 Carry out extra or different procedures

Step 2 Document findings

Step 3 Make appropriate reports (see next page)

Step 4 Consider the impact on the rest of the audit

Factors indicating the possibility of fraud include:

- previous incidents calling into question the integrity of directors
- financial reporting pressures
- weaknesses in systems
- unusual transactions
- problems in obtaining audit evidence

ISA 240.61

The auditor should determine overall responses to address the assessed risk of material misstatement due to fraud at the financial statement level and should design and perform further audit procedures whose nature, timing and extent are responsive to the assessed risk at the assertion level.

Reporting

	FRAUD	**LAW AND REGULATIONS**
To management	If suspicious, report concerns to management/audit committee ASAP	Report suspected or actual non-compliance to management/audit committee ASAP
To members	Not appropriate. However, if fraud has material impact on FS, should **modify** report	If non-compliance causes uncertainty and if it is fundamental, add emphasis of matter paragraph. If it has a material effect, modify as for fraud
To third parties	Is there a statutory duty to report? Is it in the public interest to report? Request that the directors report it. If they don't, make report to relevant authority.	

Auditors should bear in mind their professional duties of confidence and seek legal advice, if required.

Auditors must plan and perform procedures recognising that related party transactions which should be disclosed in financial statements might exist and not be disclosed.

Problems

Such transactions may not be for money (that is, they may not appear in the financial records), they may not be evident to management or auditors, they could be easily concealed by management or directors.

Auditors should:

- discuss related parties with management

- be alert for parties that could be related

- investigate unusual transactions

- review relevant evidence such as minutes of directors' meetings and statutory records

Notes

6: Audit planning

Topic List

Planning is a vital skill for an auditor, so the importance of this chapter cannot be overstated. At this stage the audit partner will need to select an audit team with suitable skills to carry out the audit.

Decisions will also need to be made as to whether the audit firm possesses all the relevant skills in-house. If not they will make use of an expert. Similarly the impact of internal audit will need to be assessed.

Sampling helps an auditor to decide how to obtain his evidence, and on which items in the financial statements.

Purpose of planning (ISA 300)

- Ensures attention devoted to important areas
- Identification and resolution of potential problems
- Work performed effectively and efficiently
- Proper assignment of work to engagement team members
- Facilitates direction/supervision of team members
- Facilitates review of work
- Allows coordination of work done by others eg. expert

The overall strategy and audit plan should be documented and updated as necessary.

Audit strategy document

Sets the scope, timing and direction of the audit and guides development of the audit plan. It involves:

- determining the characteristics of the engagement
- ascertaining the reporting objectives
- considering the important factors that will determine the focus of efforts (eg. materiality, risk)

Audit plan

This is more detailed than the audit strategy. It includes:

- description of nature, timing and extent of planned risk assessment procedures
- description of nature, timing and extent of further audit procedures at the assertion level
- other audit procedures required

The usual hierarchy of staff on an audit:

Reporting partner

Audit manager

Audit supervisor

Audit senior

Audit assistants

It is important to foster a good relationship with client staff. Relationships will be enhanced if the auditors aim to provide a high quality service that caters for the needs of the audit.

Auditors should be trying to understand what the client wants to gain from an audit and be seeking to meet that need, as well as fulfilling the audit objective.

Signs of a poor approach to client relations

- Little contact with client managers and staff
- Perceiving audit to be merely a fault finding exercise
- Failing to discuss audit findings with client staff during the audit

Certain skills and attitudes are critical to providing client service excellence.

Skills

- Communication
- Negotiation
- Interviewing

Attitudes

- Politeness
- Sensitivity to client needs
- Tidiness and orderliness

ISA 220 requires that an appropriate level of *professional scepticism* is applied by audit staff in the conduct of an audit. This does not mean doubting everything a client says but, on the other hand, also does not mean accepting everything at face value.

Direction	Supervision	Review
The audit partner should inform the audit team of: • their responsibilities • the nature of the business • potential accounting/ auditing problems • the overall audit plan A good planning meeting prior to going on site should achieve this.	The audit partner should consider: • progress • competency of audit team • significant issues arising from the audit • matters for further consideration Members of the audit team will supervise more junior members in their work.	Audit work performed will be reviewed by more senior staff on the audit team. The audit engagement partner will carry out an overall review when the audit work has been completed to ensure he is in a position to issue his opinion.

Experts

A person or firm possessing special skill, knowledge and experience in a particular field other than auditing

There are four issues for an auditor to assess.

1. Whether it is necessary to use an expert
2. Competence and objectivity of the expert
3. The expert's scope of work
4. The actual work of the expert

The following might require evidence from an expert:

Asset valuation, determination of quantity/completion of assets or of specialist amounts (eg actuarial valuation)

The auditor must consider the professional certification of the expert, his reputation, his capacity in relation to the entity (ie, employee or contracted third party)

Assess the expert's written instructions to assess: objectives/scope of work, general outline of matters covered, intended use of information, extent of the expert's access to information and files

Consider: the source data used, assumptions and methods used, the timing of the work, the results in the light of the auditor's overall understanding of the business

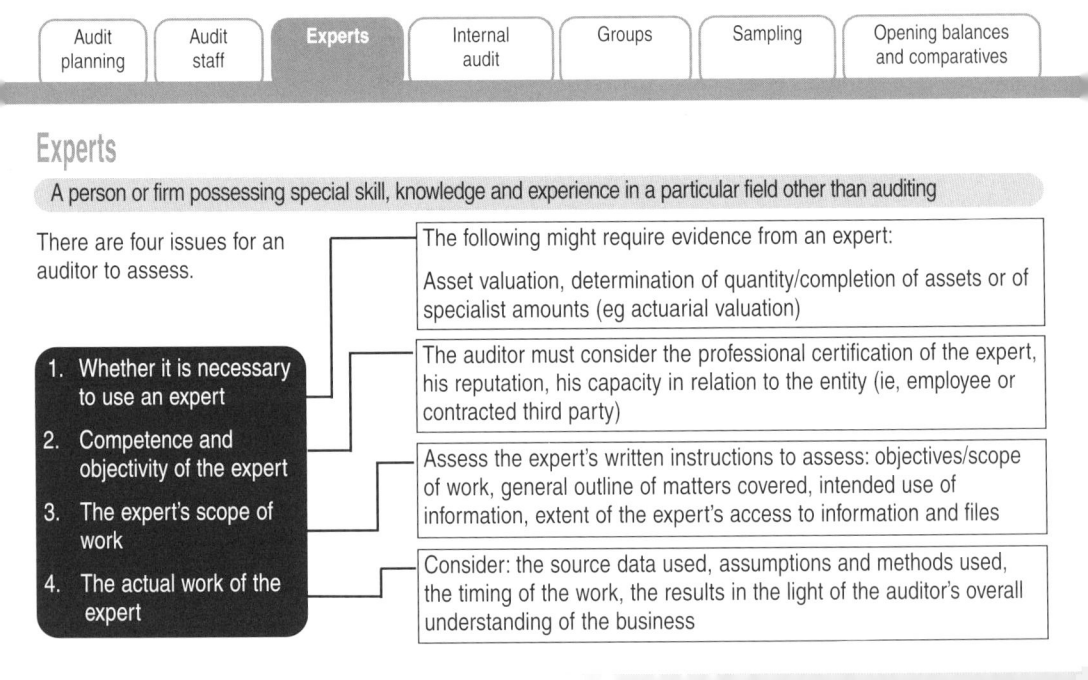

Internal audit

Internal auditors are people employed by the entity who, amongst other things, check that the internal controls in a company are operating efficiently and effectively. Only larger companies would be likely to afford an internal audit department.

- External auditors are independent of the company, internal auditors are employed by them.

- External auditors carry out a statutory audit, internal auditors do what management direct.

- External auditors report to members, internal audit to management.

Preliminary assessment

Key criteria

- Organisational status (reports directly to board?)

- Scope (types of assignments)

- Technical competence

- Professional care (is work properly planned, supervised and reviewed?)

If the internal auditor wants to use the work of the internal auditor they will need to liaise.

YOU MUST APPRECIATE THE DIFFERENCES BETWEEN INTERNAL/EXTERNAL AUDITORS.

Evaluating the work

At the planning stage, the auditors must ensure they understand the scope and role of internal audit, as part of their understanding of the business.

They may be able to make use of IA work on **internal control**.

If the auditors decide to make use of the work of internal audit, they must **evaluate** that work to ensure that it is **sufficient and appropriate** for them to base their opinion on. The table adjacent gives examples of questions which they might ask.

Have the internal auditors sufficient and adequate training to carry out the work?
Are the internal auditors proficient?
Is the work of assistants properly supervised, reviewed and documented?
Are the conclusions reached appropriate given the evidence obtained?
Are reports produced consistent with the work undertaken?
Have any unusual matters discovered by the internal audit department been resolved?
Are any amendments to the external auditors' plan necessary due to the work?
Has the external auditor sufficiently tested the work of IA to confirm that it is adequate?

Principal auditors are the auditors with the responsibility for reporting on the financial statements of an entity when those financial statements include financial information of one or more components audited by other auditors. They are required to report to members as to whether **group accounts** give a **true and fair view**. They have **sole responsibility** for that audit opinion.

Rights of principal auditors

- All standard statutory auditor rights apply

- Right to require explanations and information from UK auditors of group companies

- Right to require parent company to take reasonable steps to obtain reasonable information from group entities

Acceptance as principal auditors

- Consider the **materiality** of the segment not audited by you
- **Knowledge** of the group
- Nature of **relationship** with other audit firm
- Ability to perform additional **procedures**, if necessary
- **Risk** of material misstatements in bits audited by others

Sampling is a **key aspect of obtaining sufficient appropriate audit evidence**. A sample must be chosen which enables the auditor to get the evidence he needs.

There are four key issues.

Two testing procedures do not involve sampling:
- Testing 100% of items in a population
- Testing all items with certain characteristics

1. Design

The auditor should consider:
- the specific audit objectives
- the nature of the population
- the sampling method
- the selection method

Sampling

Applying audit procedures to < 100% of items in a population

Tolerable error

Maximum unintentional mistake in the population that auditors will accept

2. Size

Consider risk, expectations of errors and acceptable levels of errors.

The greater the reliance on the results of a list of control using audit sampling, the lower the sampling risk the auditors are willing to accept and, consequently, the larger the sample size.

3. Selection

Three main methods:

Random (all items have equal chance of selection)

Systematic (constant interval between items)

Haphazard (chosen at will, but guarding against bias in the selection)

4. Evaluation

Auditors must analyse any errors in the sample and draw inferences for the population as a whole.

Qualitative aspects of the error should be considered (nature of error/balance). Errors may be **extrapolated** against the whole balance of the population.

Opening balances

Those account balances that exist at the beginning of the period, reflecting the effect of transactions of preceding periods and its accounting policies

Auditors must obtain sufficient appropriate audit evidence that:

- opening balances b/f are right
- they do not contain misstatements material to current year figures
- accounting policies are consistently applied or adequately disclosed

Incoming auditors

Testing opening balances can be difficult for new auditors because they did not audit prior year figures. They should:

- ascertain whether prior report was unqualified
- undertake discussions with management about opening figures
- undertake substantive procedures on opening figures if concerns arise

Comparatives

The corresponding amounts from the preceding period which are part of the current year's financial statements

Continuing auditors

- Check balances b/f correctly
- If unresolved prior year problem is material to CY, qualify report due to opening balances and comparatives
- If material to CY but opening balances are not affected, report should refer to comparatives
  - Qualification
  - Explanatory paragraph

Incoming auditors: audited comparatives

- Responsible for comparatives as part of CY accounts
- Procedures as for continuing auditors

Incoming auditors: unaudited comparatives

- Ensure there is clear disclosure that the comparatives are unaudited
- Should carry out procedures as for continuing auditors, as far as possible

7: Audit of stock

In practice, stock is a very important audit area. For manufacturing businesses, it is often the largest item on the balance sheet, and is usually material.

Stock can be a difficult area to audit. It often comprises lots of small items, which can make it time consuming to audit. There are three key areas: the stock take (existence), cut off and valuation.

Sources of rules on stock

Companies Act 1985
SSAP 9
Auditing standards/guidelines re stock

Stock should be valued at the lower of cost and net realisable value.

SSAP 9 does not allow LIFO as a method of valuation.

Methods of valuation

- First in first out (FIFO)
- Last in first out (LIFO)
- Weighted average cost
- Other similar methods

Responsibilities in relation to stock

Management: ensure stock figure in FS represents stock that exists/is owned, keep stock take records.

Auditors: obtain sufficient audit evidence about stock, and attend stock take if stock is material.

The stock take

There are various methods:

The auditors' favourite

- Stock taking at the year end
- Stock taking prior to/after the year end
- Continuous stock taking

Auditors must ensure that all stock lines are counted annually, the stock records are adequate and that management investigates all material differences.

Planning stock take

Gain knowledge (previous year) and discuss major changes with management. **Assess key factors** (such as, nature of stock, high value items, accounting, location, controls). **Plan procedures** (time/location of attendance, high value items, any specialist help, third party confirmations required?)

During stock take

Check **instructions** are followed
Make **test counts** for accuracy
Check procedures for **obsolete** stock
Confirm **third party** stock separate
Conclude whether stock take has been **properly carried out**
Gain overall **impression** of stock

Review stock taking instructions

Ensure there is provision for:

Organisation of count (supervision, marking of stock, control during the process, identification of obsolete stock). **Counting** (systematic counting to ensure all stock is counted, teams of two counters one independent of stock usually). **Recording** (control over stock sheets, ink used, signed by counters).

After stock take

Trace **test count** items to final stock sheets
All count records **included** in final total?

Confirm **cut off** using final goods in and out records (see page 70)
Check replies from **third parties**
Confirm **valuation** (see page 71)

Stock movements must be recorded in the correct period.

Cut off is critical at the following points in the accounting cycle:

- Point of purchase/receipt of goods
- Raw materials going to production
- Transfer of WIP to finished goods
- Sale/despatch of finished goods

Purchase invoices should only be recorded as liabilities if goods were received prior to the stock count.

Invoices for goods despatched after the stock count should not appear in the profit and loss account in the year.

There are usually fewer problems with sales cut off than purchase cut off.

Cut off procedure at stock take

Record the relevant movements (last and first goods despatched and received numbers).

Observe whether cut off procedures are being followed during count.

Discuss procedures with management.

Cut off procedure at final audit

Match goods received notes with purchase invoices and goods despatched notes with sales invoices and ensure all in the **correct period**. Match materials requisitions with work in progress figures to ensure cut off correct.

Stock should be valued at the lower of cost and net realisable value

Original cost (All types of stock)

The various methods of valuing cost were outlined on page 68. The auditors must ensure that the **method** is **allowed** under law and standards, **consistent, calculated correctly**.

Actual costs can be checked by referring to **supplier invoices**.

The auditor should bear in mind the **age** of stock when considering cost.

Production cost (WIP and FG)

Cost is the cost of purchase + **cost of conversion**

The auditors may be able to use **analytical procedures** to assess the costs of conversion

Material: check to invoices and price lists

Labour: check to wage records/time summaries

Overheads: allocation consistent and based on normal production

NRV (All types of stock)

Auditors should compare cost/NRV. **NRV is likely to be lower** than **cost** where:

- costs increasing
- stocks deteriorated
- stock obsolete
- marketing strategy dictates
- errors made

The auditors should follow up **obsolete items** and **review prices** and strategies.

Notes

8: Audit of other assets (and related items)

Topic List

Fixed assets

Debtors

Bank and cash

You must be able to audit all the balance sheet areas. Any could come up in your assessment.

Fixed assets and debtors are particularly important areas.

Tangible fixed assets

Physical assets held for **continuing use** in the business

Internal control considerations

- Acquisitions are authorised
- Disposals are authorised
- Proceeds are accounted for
- Security over fixed assets sufficient
- Fixed assets maintained properly
- Depreciation reviewed annually
- Is a register kept?

Charges and commitments (rights)

Review statutory books for evidence of charges, examine post year end invoices and board minutes for evidence of any capital commitments.

Audit procedures

Completeness

Obtain a summary, reconcile it to last year's schedules. **Reconcile** the list of assets in the **general ledger** with those in the **fixed asset register** or list of assets. Obtain explanations for missing assets. Test some physical assets to ensure they are recorded.

Existence

Confirm that the company physically inspects all the assets in the FA register annually. **Inspect assets** (Do they exist? What's their condition? Are they in use?). Reconcile opening and closing motor vehicles by number as well as by value.

Valuation

Verify valuation to **valuation certificate** (consider reasonableness of valuation). Check any **revaluation surplus** has been **correctly calculated**. Check that revaluations are updated regularly. Ensure **disclosure** correct (P & L/STRGL).

Additions (rights/valuation/completeness)

Check **additions** to **invoices**/architect's certificates etc. Check purchases **properly allocated** to fixed asset accounts and authorised by correct person and that all additions have been **recorded** in the general ledger and the fixed asset register.

Depreciation (valuation)

Review depreciation rates in light of: asset lives, residual values, replacement policy, past experience (consistency), possible obsolescence. **Check that depreciation has been charged** on all assets with a useful economic life. **Check calculation**. Ensure depreciation not charged on fully depreciated assets. Check that rates & policies are disclosed in the FS. Check that depreciation on revalued assets is based on the revalued amount.

Ownership

Verify title to **land** by checking **title deeds/leases**. Obtain certificate from people holding deeds to confirm why they are held. Inspect **registration documents for vehicles**, confirm that they are **used for the business**. Examine documents of title for other assets.

Disposals (rights/completeness/occurrence /accuracy)

Verify disposals to **sales documentation** (invoice) and check **calculation of profit**/loss is correct. Check that disposals are **authorised** and proceeds are reasonable. Ensure that asset is no longer used as security.

Insurance (valuation)

Review insurance policies in force for all assets to ensure cover is sufficient and check expiry dates.

Investments include:

- listed investments
- unlisted investments

(This may include subsidiaries and associates.)

Existence

- Examine certificates of title
- Third party confirmations
- Transfer documents
- Purchase invoices/contracts
- Sales invoices

Valuation

- Refer to FT or Daily lists
- Check for falls in value post y/e
- Review accounts of unlisted investments (net assets value/reasonable)

Investment income

- Ensure only recognised when appropriate

Completeness/occurrence/accuracy

- Check all income received
- Review for unusual entries

Intangible fixed assets

General intangibles

Types of asset include patents, licences, trade marks, development costs, and goodwill. Intangibles have a finite useful life and should be amortised.

Audit tests:
- Prepare analysis of movements
- Obtain any third party confirmations
- Review specialist valuations
- Inspect purchase documentation
- Confirm authorisation
- Check computation of amortisation
- Review sales returns for income

Development costs

The criteria for allowing development costs to be capitalised are:
- project clearly defined
- expenditure separately identifiable
- outcome reasonably certain (3 factors)
- resources exist to make it commercial

Audit tests reflect these criteria:
- Check accounting records
- Review market research
- Review budgets/forecast cash
- Check amortisation

In other words, ensure that the criteria are met and disclosure is correct.

Debtors' listing/age analysis

Much of the detailed work will be carried out on a sample of **debtors' balances** chosen from a list of **sales ledger balances**. Ideally, this will be **aged**, showing amounts owed and from when they are owed. The following work should be done **(completeness)**.

- Check balances from sales ledger to list of balances and vice versa
- Check the total of the list to the sales ledger control account
- Add up the list of balances to ensure it is correct
- Confirm whether the list reconciles to the sales ledger control account

Circularisation

Verification of trade debtors by direct circularisation is the normal method of getting audit evidence to check the **existence** and **rights and obligations** of trade debtors.

Positive circularisation: debtor is requested to confirm the accuracy of the balance shown or state in what respect he is in disagreement (preferable method).

Negative circularisation: debtor is requested only to reply if the amount is disputed.

The circularisation letter is generally **prepared by the client**, but should be **sent back to the auditor** by the debtor.

Sample selection

Special attention to:

- **old** unpaid accounts
- accounts **written off** in period
- accounts with **credit** balances
- accounts settled by **round sum payments**

Do not overlook:

- **nil balances**
- accounts paid by the time of the audit

Follow up, where:

- debtors disagree with the balance
- debtors do not respond (positive method only)

Reasons for disagreements: disputes, cut off problems, receipt send before year end but received afterwards, mis-posting, customers netting off credits and debits, teeming and lading frauds. The **auditors should investigate** the reasons for disagreement.

Alternative procedures (where no response arrives)

Second (& third) requests should be sent to the debtor in the first instance. Then the auditors should involve credit controller to chase the debt, and do other tests.

Auditor may check the receipt of cash after date, verify purchase orders, and test the company's control over bad debts (see below).

Bad debts

This is to test the valuation of trade debtors in the balance sheet. A significant test is reviewing all the **cash received after date** (which gives evidence on the **collectability** of debts).

Procedures

Confirm adequacy of provision by **reviewing customer** correspondence/discussion with the credit controller. Examine customer files for overdue debts and consider whether provision is sufficient

Review correspondence with **solicitors** in case legal action is being taken to enforce debts

Examine **credit notes** issued after the year end and ensure those relating to invoices in the relevant period have been provided for

Investigate all **unusual items** in the sales ledger, for example, credit balances

Prepayments

- Verify by reference to the cash book/expense invoices/correspondence etc
- Check the calculation
- Review for reasonableness and do analytical review with prior year

Sales

Debtors will often be tested in conjunction with sales.

Completeness and occurrence

Analytical review is likely to be important.

Consider:

- level of sales, year on year
- effect of changing quantities sold
- effect of changing prices
- levels of goods returned/discounts
- efficiency of labour/sales

Accuracy

Check:

- pricing/additions on invoices
- discounts properly calculated
- VAT added correctly
- casts in sales ledger
- control account reconciliation

Also, trace debits in sales ledger to credit notes

Sales cut off   (Goods in stock are not also treated as sales in the year)

Check goods despatched and returns inward around the year end to ensure:

- invoices/credit notes dated in the same period
- invoices/credit notes posted to the sales ledger in the same period

Review the sales ledger control account for unusual items near the year end and review material after-date invoices and credit notes to see if in correct period

Bank

[Bank address]

Dear Sirs,

In accordance with the agreed practice for provision of information to auditors, please forward information on our mutual client(s) as detailed below on behalf of the bank, its branches and subsidiaries. This request and your response will not create any contractual or other duty with us.

Parent Company Ltd
Subsidiary 1 Ltd

AUDIT CONFIRMATION DATE (30 APRIL 20X6)

Information required	Tick
Standard	
Trade finance	

The audit of bank will need to cover **completeness, existence, rights and obligations**, and **valuation**.

All these elements can be audited through the **bank letter** (example to the left). This is a standard document.

Banks will require:

- explicit written authority from client
- auditors' request must refer to it
- request must reach the bank two weeks before the year end

The auditors must beware **'window dressing'**, that is, recognising cash receipts actually received after date, and recording cheques not paid, not sending them out until after year end.

Derivative and commodity trading
Custodian arrangements
Other information (see attached)

The authority to disclose information signed by your customer is attached / already held by you (delete as appropriate). Please advise us if this authority is insufficient for you to provide full disclosure of the information requested.

The contract name is [John Caller]
Telephone [01 234 5678]

Yours faithfully,
[XXX Accountants]

Procedures

- Obtain bank confirmations
- Check the maths of the bank reconciliation
- Trace cheques shown as outstanding to the after date bank statements
- Trace receipts shown as outstanding to after date bank statements
- Review previous bank reconciliation to ensure all amounts are cleared
- Obtain explanations for items in bank statements, not cash book and vice versa
- Verify balances on reconciliation to bank letter and cash book
- Scrutinise the cash book for unusual items

If cash balances at the client are **material**, then the auditor may attend a cash count. Procedures are similar to those for a stock count in many ways.

Planning

Document on file: the time and location of the count, who is to be present (audit and client staff). **Ensure** that the cash book are written up to date and in ink.

During the cash count

- Count cash balances held in front of official responsible. (The auditor should never be left alone with the cash)
- Enquire into any IOUs
- Confirm cash balances agree with the FS

After the cash count

- Ensure that certificates of cash in hand are obtained as appropriate
- Ensure unbanked cheques are subsequently banked/agree to bank reconciliation
- Ensure IOUs have been reimbursed
- Ensure IOUs/cashed cheques outstanding for too long have been provided for
- Ensure all balances counted are reflected in the accounts

9: Audit of liabilities (and related items)

Topic List

Current liabilities and purchases

Long-term liabilities

Accounting estimates

Share capital

Statutory books

This chapter covers a number of liabilities which a company might have. The auditor must consider the possibility of understatement of creditors, particularly if the client has liquidity problems, or is seeking further credit from someone, for example, the bank.

Suppliers and lenders are a good source of external evidence. Auditors may also test purchases by using analytical procedures.

Auditors should be aware of the possibility of understatement of creditors

There are **two detailed objectives** with regard to trade creditors:

- Is cut off correct between goods received and invoices received?
- Do trade creditors represent the *bona fide* amounts due by the company?

Trade creditors' listing

Check that the listing has been extracted correctly from the purchase ledger

Reconcile the total with the purchase ledger control account

Check that the list of balance adds up

Completeness, rights and obligations, existence

The key test is a comparison of **supplier statements** with the purchase ledger balances. Supplier statements are third party evidence.

However, it is sometimes necessary to **circularise creditors**. Examples of such situations are:

- supplier statements are unavailable/incomplete
- internal controls are weak and material misstatement of liabilities is feared as a consequence
- suspicion that client is understating deliberately

Purchases and expenses

Occurrence/completeness

Analytical procedures are important. Consider:

- level of purchases/expenses month by month
- effect of quantities purchased
- effect of changing prices
- ratio of purchases to trade creditors
- ratio of trade creditors to stock

Additional tests include tracing purchases and other expenses from the nominal ledger to the purchase ledger and invoices. Are they valid for the company/authorised?

Cut off

Check from the **last goods received note** (from stock take) to the ledger or list of accruals.

Review the **schedule of accruals** to check that goods received after the year end are not included.

Review invoices and credit notes after the year end to ensure that those relating to prior year are included.

Reconcile batch postings around the year end, to ensure that invoices are posted in the correct period.

Accruals

As a general rule, accruals lend themselves to being audited by **analytical review** as they should be comparable to prior years. Other substantive procedures are noted here.

General accruals (completeness and valuation)

- Check calculation of accruals and trace back to supporting documentation
- Review ledger accounts to ensure all accruals have been included
- Scrutinise post year end payments to see if any should have been accrued
- Consider basis for round sum accruals (comparable to last year?)

PAYE/VAT (completeness and valuation)

PAYE: Likely to be one month's deductions. Check amount paid to the Revenue
VAT: Check reasonableness to next return. Verify amount paid in year to cashbook

Wages and salaries (completeness and valuation)

Analytical review will give some assurance on pay creditors. However, auditors may also carry out tests such as: checking remuneration per payroll to personnel records, confirm existence of employees by meeting them, check calculations on the payroll, check validity of deductions to supporting documentation. Confirm net pay to bank.

Long term liabilities

Those due after more than one year. Usually they are debentures, loan stock and things like bank loans.

The key financial statement assertions are:

- **completeness:** whether all long term liabilities have been disclosed
- **accuracy:** whether interest payable has been calculated correctly and included in the right period
- **disclosure:** whether long term loans are correctly disclosed

Procedures

- Obtain/prepare a schedule of loans
- Agree opening balances to prior year and check the adds
- Compare the balances to the general ledger
- Check lenders to any register of lenders (eg debenture holders)
- Trace additions and repayments to cash book
- Confirm repayment conforms to agreement
- Verify borrowing limits per the articles are not exceeded
- Obtain direct confirmation from lenders
- Review minutes and cash book to ensure that all loans have been included

Accounting estimate

An approximation of the amount of an item in the absence of precise means of measurement

Allowances to reduce stock/debtors to their estimated realisable value, depreciation, accrued revenue, provision for a lawsuit, construction contracts or warranty claims

2. Audit procedures

Auditors should gain an understanding of the estimation process. They should also:

- consider reasonableness (based on what?)
- seek external evidence about the estimate
- consider whether an expert opinion needed
- test the calculations for arithmetic
- compare the estimates with previous ones

1. Nature

Often these estimates are based on a formula based on past experience.

3. Evaluation

They should make a final decision on reasonableness based on other evidence from audit.

Share capital

Auditors should ensure that the directors have observed their legal duties in regard to share capital and reserves (for example, not distributed undistributable reserves and observed pre-emption rights when issuing shares).

Key procedures

Agree authorised share capital to the memorandum. Verify share transfer details and cash payments to cash book. Agree dividends paid to cash book and to the minutes of the AGM where the dividend was proposed. Check calculation of movement on reserves.

Statutory books

Verify that the disclosures made in the FS agree to the statutory books and that the books agree to the returns made to the Registrar. Have the statutory books been maintained/updated properly? Consider whether the accounting records are sufficient to fulfil the directors' legal duties.

10: Audit completion and reporting

Topic List

Overall review

Subsequent events

Going concern

Management representations

Audit reports

Modified reports

Other information

The auditor carries out a number of reviews at the end of an audit. He needs to ensure that the accounts stack up, that the opening and comparative positions are fair and that the information is consistent with other information given in the annual report.

Other reviews, such as going concern and subsequent events are very important. The post balance sheet period is vital for the auditor in the collection of evidence.

In your assessment you may be required to:

■   *describe to a junior member of staff how a particular modification differs from the standard report*

■   *give extracts from the audit reports*

You should be comfortable with the various reports.

Towards the end of their audit, the auditors should review the financial statements to ensure that they are reasonable, and consistent with evidence obtained, so that they can draw a conclusion on truth and fairness.

1. Accounting regulations

The auditors should **examine the accounting policies**, considering: what policies are usually adopted in the industry, whether there is substantial authoritative support for the policy, whether departures are necessary for a true and fair view, whether the FS reflect the substance of the underlying transactions.

Some accounting standards allow a **choice of methods**, which often have a material effect.

2. Consistency and reasonableness

- Do FS adequately reflect **explanations** received?

- Are there any **new factors** in presentation?

- Do **analytical procedures** produce expected results?

- Has the **presentation** been unduly affected by directors' wishes?

- What is the potential impact of **unadjusted errors**?

		P & L account		Balance sheet	
	20X2	Dr	Cr	Dr	Cr
		£	£	£	£
(a)	ABC Ltd debt unprovided				
(b)	Opening/closing stock under-valued*	10,470			10,470
(c)	Closing stock undervalued	21,540			
(d)	Opening unaccrued expense		34,105	34,105	21,540
	Telephone*				
	Electricity*		453	453	
(e)	Closing unaccrued expenses		905	905	
	Telephone	427			427
	Electricity	1,128			1,128
(f)	Obsolete stock write off	2,528			2,528
Total		36,093	35,463	35,463	36,093
	*Cancelling items	21,540			21,540
			453	453	
			905	905	
		14,553	34,105	34,105	14,553

> The auditors should summarise unadjusted (immaterial) errors and consider the materiality and the potential effect of adjusting them.
>
> It should include their best estimate of errors are unavailable.
>
> They may ask the directors to adjust. If they refuse: consider the impact on the audit report.

Auditors carry out their audit some time later than the date of financial statements.

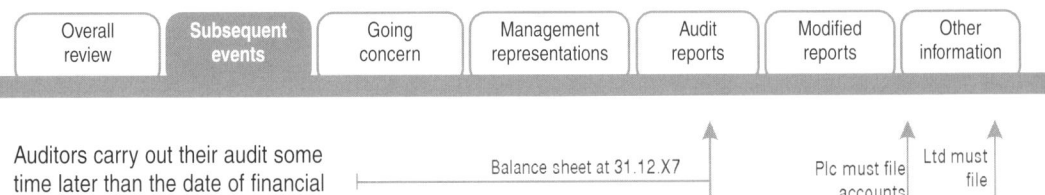

Balance sheet at 31.12.X7

Profit and loss account to 31.12.X7

| J | F | M | A | M | J | J | A | S | O | N | D | J | F | M | A | M | J | J | A | S | O |

Plc must file accounts

Ltd must file accounts

Audit carried out in this period

Auditors must ensure that things happening between the balance sheet date and the date of their report do not make the financial statements not give a true and fair view.

Example

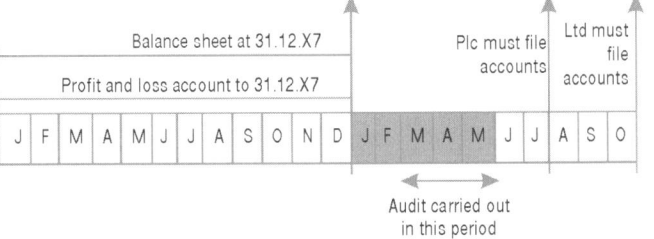

Debtors owes company money at 31.12.X7 → 2nd February debtors becomes bankrupt → Debt not recoverable

Prior to the audit report being signed

Auditors should carry out procedures to obtain evidence PBSE, including: enquiries of management, reading minutes of directors' meetings, reviewing most recent financial information.

After the audit report has been signed

Auditors should carry out additional procedures and issue a new report if necessary.

Examples: enquiries of management

- What is the status of items involving subjective data included in the FS?
- Are there any new commitments (borrowing/guarantees) in the new year?
- Have there been any issues of capital?
- Have there been any major events?
- Are there any unusual accounting treatment adjustments?

Going concern assumption

An entity is ordinarily viewed as continuing in business for the foreseeable future with neither the intention nor the necessity of liquidation, ceasing trading or seeking protection from its creditors.

ISA 570 *Going concern* gives guidance.

1. Management responsibility

As going concern is a fundamental principle management has a responsibility to assess the entity's ability to continue as a going concern.

2. Auditor responsibilities

The auditors are responsible for considering the appropriateness of management's use of the going concern assumption, and the existence of any material uncertainties in relation to going concern which should be disclosed in the FS.

3. Planning and risk assessment

In obtaining an understanding of the entity, the auditor should consider whether anything casts doubt on the entity's going concern status. If management have undertaken a preliminary assessment of going concern, the auditor should review it. The auditor should remain alert throughout the audit for any factors which would indicate problems (examples given below).

Financial

- Net liabilities
- Debt restructuring/renegotiation
- Negative operating cashflows
- Adverse financial ratios
- Substantial operating losses
- Inability to pay creditors
- Substantial sales of fixed assets

Operating

- Loss of key management/staff/markets/franchise
- Technical developments rendering key products obsolete

Other

- Major legal proceedings/non-compliance
- Changes in legislation

4. Evaluation

The auditor should evaluate management's assessment of the entity's ability to continue as a going concern. Matters include:

- the period assessed by management (see 5)
- the system of risk id
- budgets/forecasts/cashflows
- whether assumptions appropriate
- sensitivity of budgets/forecasts to change
- obligations/guarantees
- existence/adequacy/terms of borrowing facilities
- plans by management for resolving matters giving rise to concern (if any)

5. Foreseeable future

- If management's assessment of the entity's ability to continue covers **less than twelve months from the balance sheet date** the auditor should ask management to **extend** its assessment period

- If the period used in the going concern assessment is **less than one year from the date of approval** of the financial statements and this has not been disclosed, the auditor should **disclose** this in the current report

6. Further procedures

When events are identified which may cast significant doubt on the entity's ability to continue the auditor should:

- review management's plans for future action

- carry out audit procedures to confirm or dispel whether or not a material uncertainty exists (eg analysing/discussing cashflow/profit forecasts with management, reviewing terms of debentures/loans, reading minutes of shareholder meetings, reviewing events after the period end)

- seek written representations from management regarding future plans

7. Reporting

Going concern assumption appropriate but a material uncertainty exists

- If **adequate** disclosure is made the auditor should express an **unqualified opinion** but include an **emphasis of matter paragraph** (explanatory paragraph) highlighting the issue

- If disclosure is **inadequate** the auditor should express a **qualified** or **adverse** opinion (and make specific reference to the material uncertainty)

Disclosure

'Adequate' disclosures are as follows.

- Statement re GC
- Pertinent facts
- Nature of concern
- Statement of directors' assumptions
- Plans for resolution
- Actions by directors

Going concern assumption inappropriate

If the financial statements have been prepared on a going concern basis the auditor should express an **adverse** opinion.

Auditors receive many **representations** from management during the course of an audit, and **some may be critical** to obtaining sufficient, appropriate audit evidence. An example, which the auditors must get, is acknowledgement from the directors of their responsibility for the financial statements which the auditors have audited.

Guidance is given in ISA 580 *Management representations*

Form of written confirmations

Representation letter from management

Letter from the auditors acknowledged in writing by the directors

Minutes of meeting where such a letter was approved

1. Representations by management as audit evidence

ISA 580.2 Auditors should obtain appropriate representation from management. (This should be obtained before the audit report is issued.)

When auditors receive such representations they should:

- seek **corroborative evidence**
- evaluate whether the representations seem consistent/reasonable
- consider whether the individuals involved should be reasonably informed

There are only two times where management representations may be the only source of evidence available to the auditor:

- Where knowledge of the facts is confined to management
- Where the matter is principally one of judgement or opinion

2. Basic elements of a management representation letter

The letter should be: addressed to the auditors, contain specified information, appropriately dated, approved by those who have the specific knowledge. Auditors will normally request that the letter is discussed by the board and signed by the chairman.

3. If management refuse to sign

If management refuse to sign the management representation letter, the auditor should consider whether they should rely on other (less significant) representations made during the audit.

We looked at an example of an unqualified audit report in Chapter 2.

EXPLICIT OPINIONS	IMPLIED OPINIONS	
In the balance sheet, of the **state of the company's affairs** at the end of the financial year	**Proper accounting records** have been kept and proper returns adequate for the audit received from branches not visited.	
	The **accounts** are in **agreement** with the **accounting records** and returns.	
In the profit and loss account, of the **company's profit or loss** for the financial year	**All information** and explanations have been **received** as the auditors think necessary and they have had access at all times to the company's books, accounts and vouchers.	
	Details of **directors' emoluments** and other benefits have been correctly **disclosed** in the FS.	
	Particulars of loans and other **transactions** in favour of **directors** and others have been correctly **disclosed** in the FS.	

A recent change in the Companies Act now requires auditors to state in their report whether in their opinion the information given in the Directors' Report is consistent with the accounts.

(The standard UK audit report – see pg 6-7 has not been updated yet for this change.)

| Overall review | Subsequent events | Going concern | Management representations | Audit reports | **Modified reports** | Other information |

Matters that do affect the auditor's opinion.

Limitation on scope

Examples

Where the auditor cannot receive all the information and explanations necessary to his audit, eg absence of accounting records, because of accident or concealment, failure by management to provide written representations

If material:

...'Except for...might' **qualified** opinion, where auditors disclaim the opinion on a particular aspect of financial statements.

If pervasive:

Disclaimer of opinion given, where auditors state they are unable to form an opinion.

Must explain what evidence they were looking for and what possible effect the matter for which they have no evidence might have on FS.

Matters that do affect the auditor's opinion.

Disagreement

Examples

Circumstances giving rise to **disagreement** might include: inappropriate accounting policies, disagreement over facts/figures in the FS, disagreement over level of disclosure in the FS, failure to comply with relevant legislation or other requirements.

If material:

...'Except for' **qualified** opinion, where auditors disagree with one material aspect of the financial statements.

If pervasive:

Adverse opinion (that is, the account do not give a true and fair view) given, if the disagreement substantially affects the true and fair view.

Matters that do not affect the auditor's opinon.

In certain circumstances, an auditor's report may be modified by adding an **emphasis of matter paragraph** to highlight a matter affecting the financial statements which is included in a note to the financial statements that more extensively discusses the matter. The addition of such an emphasis of matter paragraph does not affect the auditor's opinion. The auditor may also modify the auditors' report by using an emphasis of matter paragraph(s) to report matters other than those affecting the financial statements.

The ISA distinguished between **going concern** and other significant uncertainties. An example paragraph relating to going concern is laid out in the relevant standard.

The emphasis of matter paragraph should include:

- a description of the matter giving rise to the significant uncertainty

- its possible effects on the financial statements

- quantification of effect (where practicable). Where it is not possible to quantify the potential effects this should be stated